Hobnob the Troll

Written by Mike Jubb

Illustrated by Mike Lester

Hobnob the Troll can rock and roll.
He can swing along and sing a song . . .

but Hobnob cannot fly.

Hobnob the Troll can rock and roll.
He can hop and jog like a frog on a log . . .

but Hobnob cannot fly.

Hobnob the Troll can rock and roll.
He can spring like a fox or a jack-in-the-box . . .

but Hobnob cannot fly.

Hobnob the Troll can rock and roll.
He can swing like a king on a long strong string . . .

but Hobnob cannot fly.

Hobnob the Troll can rock and roll.
He can hop and bop till he has to stop . . .

but Hobnob cannot fly.

Hobnob the Troll can rock and roll.
He can clip-clip-clop till he falls down flop . . .

but Hobnob cannot fly.

Hobnob the Troll can rock and roll.
He can huff and puff like a Billy Goat Gruff—

Now Hobnob the Troll can fly!